BLAZERS™

HORSEPOWER

FORMULA ONE CARS

by Sarah L. Schuette

Reading Consultant:
Barbara J. Fox
Reading Specialist
North Carolina State University

Capstone press®

Mankato, Minnesota

Blazers is published by Capstone Press,
151 Good Counsel Drive, P.O. Box 669, Mankato, Minnesota 56002.
www.capstonepress.com

Library of Congress Cataloging-in-Publication Data
Schuette, Sarah L., 1976–
    Formula One cars / by Sarah L. Schuette.
       p. cm.—(Blazers. Horsepower)
    Summary: "Brief text describes Formula One cars, including their
main features, races, and drivers"—Provided by publisher.
    Includes bibliographical references and index.
    ISBN 13: 978-0-7368-6448-0 (hardcover)
    ISBN 10: 0-7368-6448-2 (hardcover)
    1. Formula One automobiles—Juvenile literature. 2. Grand Prix
racing—Juvenile literature. I. Title. II. Series.
    TL236.S36 2007
    629.228—dc22   2005037736

Editorial Credits
Carrie A. Braulick, editor; Jason Knudson, set designer; Thomas
    Emery and Patrick D. Dentinger, book designers; Jo Miller, photo
    researcher; Scott Thoms, photo editor

Photo Credits
Artemis Images, 27
Corbis/Marcelo del Pozo, 23; NewSport/SI/Simon Bruty, 28–29;
    Reuters/Carlos Barria, cover; Reuters/China Photos, 25; Reuters/
    Paulo Whitaker, 20–21; Schlegelmilch, 11, 12, 13, 14, 16–17
Getty Images Inc./Clive Rose, 8; Mark Thompson, 22
SportsChrome Inc./Bongarts, 5, 6, 7, 26
Zuma Press/Icon SMI/Jeff Lewis, 19

**Capstone Press thanks Betty Carlan, Research Librarian, International
Motorsports Hall of Fame, Talladega, Alabama, for her assistance in
preparing this book.**

1 2 3 4 5 6 11 10 09 08 07 06

TABLE OF CONTENTS

BATTLING FOR THE LEAD

Formula One (F1) cars roll toward the starting line. When the red lights go out, the cars fly like rockets down the track.

5

Lap after lap, drivers swerve and pass. They speed around corners and blast down the straightaways. Michael Schumacher takes the lead in his red Ferrari.

The other cars can't catch up. The checkered flag waves. We have a winner!

BLAZER FACT

Michael Schumacher is one of the top F1 drivers. He has won seven world championship titles.

DESIGN

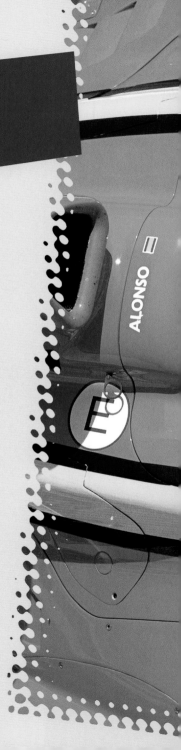

F1 cars are lightweight and small. The driver squeezes into a cockpit, or tub. The cockpit is made of strong material that protects the driver in a crash.

F1 cars have wings on the front and back. The wings push the cars down on the track. They help the cars speed around corners.

Wing

Wing

BLAZER FACT

An F1 racetrack is called a circuit. Each race is called a grand prix.

14

Although F1 cars are small, their engines are large. The engines power the cars to top speeds of about 200 miles (300 kilometers) per hour.

BLAZER FACT

Because F1 engines work so hard, they wear out quickly. They are replaced often.

F1 Car Parts

Wing

Tire

Wing

Cockpit

CREDIT SUISSE

12

MAGNETI MARELLI

CREDIT SUISSE

CREDIT SUISSE

Chassis

IMPROVING F1 CARS

Race teams never stop making their cars better and faster. They make quick tune-ups during pit stops.

When a race season is over,
race teams rebuild their cars. They
replace old parts with new ones.
They may change the car chassis,
or frame.

BLAZER FACT

The high cost of parts makes F1 racing one of the most expensive motorsports in the world.

A small design mistake can make a big difference on race day. Teams test their cars before races. Driving on road courses tests a car's speed and handling.

F1 FUTURE

Most F1 races are held in
Europe. But new racetracks
continue to be built in other
parts of the world. China has
one of the newest tracks.

F1 racing rules change often. Race organizers want to keep the sport both safe and exciting to watch. Get ready for more fast-paced F1 action!

SPEEDING DOWN THE TRACK!

GLOSSARY

chassis (CHASS-ee)—the frame on which the body of a vehicle is built

circuit (SUR-kit)—a Formula One racetrack

cockpit (KOK-pit)—the area where the driver sits in a Formula One car; the cockpit is also called a tub.

lap (LAP)—one time around a racetrack

pit stop (PIT STOP)—when a driver stops during a race so the pit crew can make adjustments, change the tires, and add fuel

road course (ROHD KORSS)—a racetrack that has an irregular shape and includes left and right turns

straightaway (STRAYT-uh-way)—the straight section of a racetrack

tune-up (TOON-up)—a small change to increase the performance of a Formula One car

wing (WING)—a long, flat panel on the front or back of a Formula One car

READ MORE

Herran, Joe, and Ron Thomas. *Formula One Car Racing*. Action Sports. Philadelphia: Chelsea House, 2003.

Piehl, Janet. *Formula One Race Cars*. Mighty Movers. Minneapolis: Lerner, 2004.

Schaefer, A. R. *Formula One Cars*. Wild Rides! Mankato, Minn.: Capstone Press, 2005.

INTERNET SITES

FactHound offers a safe, fun way to find Internet sites related to this book. All of the sites on FactHound have been researched by our staff.

Here's how:

1. Visit *www.facthound.com*

2. Choose your grade level.

3. Type in this book ID **0736864482** for age-appropriate sites. You may also browse subjects by clicking on letters, or by clicking on pictures and words.

4. Click on the **Fetch It** button.

FactHound will fetch the best sites for you!

INDEX